This Book

Belongs To

Hello!

If you Find

THIS BOOK

USEFUL

Then PLEASE

LEAVE A

Review

Date _____   Sun ▨ Mon ▨ Tue ▨ Wed ▨ Thu ▨ Fri ▨ Sat ▨

Date _____   Sun ▨ Mon ▨ Tue ▨ Wed ▨ Thu ▨ Fri ▨ Sat ▨

Date _____   Sun ▨ Mon ▨ Tue ▨ Wed ▨ Thu ▨ Fri ▨ Sat ▨

Date _____   Sun ▨ Mon ▨ Tue ▨ Wed ▨ Thu ▨ Fri ▨ Sat ▨

Date _____   Sun ▨ Mon ▨ Tue ▨ Wed ▨ Thu ▨ Fri ▨ Sat ▨

Date _____   Sun ▪ Mon ▪ Tue ▪ Wed ▪ Thu ▪ Fri ▪ Sat ▪

Date _____   Sun ▨ Mon ▨ Tue ▨ Wed ▨ Thu ▨ Fri ▨ Sat ▨

Date _____ Sun ▨ Mon ▨ Tue ▨ Wed ▨ Thu ▨ Fri ▨ Sat ▨

Date _____   Sun ▢ Mon ▢ Tue ▢ Wed ▢ Thu ▢ Fri ▢ Sat ▢

Date _____   Sun ▨ Mon ▨ Tue ▨ Wed ▨ Thu ▨ Fri ▨ Sat ▨

Date _____   Sun ▪ Mon ▪ Tue ▪ Wed ▪ Thu ▪ Fri ▪ Sat ▪

Date _____   Sun ▨ Mon ▨ Tue ▨ Wed ▨ Thu ▨ Fri ▨ Sat ▨

Date _____   Sun ▨ Mon ▨ Tue ▨ Wed ▨ Thu ▨ Fri ▨ Sat ▨

Date _____   Sun ▦ Mon ▦ Tue ▦ Wed ▦ Thu ▦ Fri ▦ Sat ▦

Date _____ Sun ▦ Mon ▦ Tue ▦ Wed ▦ Thu ▦ Fri ▦ Sat ▦

Date _____   Sun ▨ Mon ▨ Tue ▨ Wed ▨ Thu ▨ Fri ▨ Sat ▨

Date _____   Sun ▪ Mon ▪ Tue ▪ Wed ▪ Thu ▪ Fri ▪ Sat ▪

Date _____   Sun ▧ Mon ▧ Tue ▧ Wed ▧ Thu ▧ Fri ▧ Sat ▧

Date _____   Sun ▨ Mon ▨ Tue ▨ Wed ▨ Thu ▨ Fri ▨ Sat ▨

Date _____   Sun ▨ Mon ▨ Tue ▨ Wed ▨ Thu ▨ Fri ▨ Sat ▨

Date _____   Sun ▪ Mon ▪ Tue ▪ Wed ▪ Thu ▪ Fri ▪ Sat ▪

Date _____   Sun ☐ Mon ☐ Tue ☐ Wed ☐ Thu ☐ Fri ☐ Sat ☐

Date _____   Sun ■ Mon ■ Tue ■ Wed ■ Thu ■ Fri ■ Sat ■

Date _____ Sun ▨ Mon ▨ Tue ▨ Wed ▨ Thu ▨ Fri ▨ Sat ▨

Date _____   Sun ▨ Mon ▨ Tue ▨ Wed ▨ Thu ▨ Fri ▨ Sat ▨

Date _____   Sun ▢ Mon ▢ Tue ▢ Wed ▢ Thu ▢ Fri ▢ Sat ▢

Date _____   Sun ▥ Mon ▥ Tue ▥ Wed ▥ Thu ▥ Fri ▥ Sat ▥

Date _____   Sun ☐ Mon ☐ Tue ☐ Wed ☐ Thu ☐ Fri ☐ Sat ☐

GIFT THESE NOTEBOOKS TO YOUR DEAR ONES AT ANY TIME

ON THE FOLLOWING FEW PAGES, YOU WILL FIND SOME OF OUR HILARIOUS, FUNNY, AND EYE CATCHING GLOSSY COVERED NOTEBOOKS THAT YOU CAN <u>GIFT TO YOUR FRIENDS, FAMILY MEMBERS, RELATIVES, COWORKERS, OR ANYONE YOU CARE ABOUT,</u> ON CHRISTMAS, BIRTHDAY, HOLIDAY, OR ANY OTHER OCCASION.

IF YOU HAVE LIKED THIS NOTEBOOK, THEN YOU WILL LOVE THOSE AS WELL.

WE HIGHLY RECOMMEND YOU TO SEE EACH COVER AND IF SOMETHING GRABS YOUR ATTENTION, THEN PLEASE COPY THE ISBN (13 DIGIT NUMBER) THAT YOU WILL SEE UNDER EACH COVER. YOU CAN ORDER ALL THESE UNIQUE ATTENTION-GRABBING NOTEBOOKS FROM AMAZON. JUST TYPE THOSE NUMERICAL VALUES CORRECTLY IN AMAZON'S SEARCH BOX.

REST ASSURED ANYONE WILL LOVE TO HAVE THESE CUTE NOTEBOOKS.

APPROPRIATE FOR ANYONE ON ANY OCCASION

SOMETIMES YOU FORGET YOU'RE TRULY **AWESOME** SO THIS IS YOUR **REMINDER**

9798755339490

SOMETIMES YOU FORGET THAT YOU'RE **AMAZING** SO THIS IS YOUR **REMINDER**

9798755339407

YOU ALWAYS FORGET THAT YOU ARE **FANTABULOUS** SO THIS IS YOUR **REMINDER**

9798755339360

ALWAYS REMEMBER YOU ARE AWESOME

9798758428719

GIFT FOR FAMILY MEMBERS AND RELATIVES

WORLD'S BEST MOM

9798757388670

DAD YOU ARE MY KING My First Love MY FOREVER HERO

9798757408798

Best Sister EVER

9798756840360

WANNA TRADE BROTHER FOR CANDY

9798757484686

GRANDMA IS MY NAME SPOILING IS MY GAME

9798757433073

GRANDPA & GRANDCHILDREN BEST FRIENDS FOR LIFE

9798757441658

WORLD'S BEST ★AUNT★

9798757591643

I NEVER DREAMED I'D BE A SUPER COOL UNCLE BUT HERE I AM KILLING IT

9798757599786

Love YOU -MOM-

9798757388663

SADLY YOUR OTHER CHILDREN DIDN'T TURN OUT LIKE ME

9798758222973

Best Mother IN LAW

9798758413142

SUPER NANA

9798757404967

FUNNY GAG GIFTS TO MAKE ANYONE LAUGH

ALL MY SHIT IDEAS

9798497046984

LIFE IS A BOWL OF SOUP I'M A FREAKING FORK

9798497052220

OUR FAVORITE FAMILY ROAD TRIP GAME IS "HEATED ARGUMENT"

9798497771008

I USE THIS NOTEBOOK WHILE I AM REALLY TOO HIGH

9798497046953

SERIOUSLY? DESPITE THIS LOOK ON MY FACE, YOU ARE STILL TALKING!

9798497052114

LET ME STOP DOING EVERYTHING TO WORK ON YOUR PROBLEM

9798497057348

I'D GIVE YOU A FUNNY GIFT BUT AT YOUR AGE YOU WILL PISS YOURSELF

9798757639666

FEW PEOPLE NEED HIGH FIVE:
- IN THE FACE
- WITH A CHAIR
- MADE OF STEEL

9798497771046

MY 3 FAVORITE THINGS ARE:
EATNG MY PARENTS AND NOT USING COMMAS

9798497736021

"IF YOU FALL, DON'T WORRY I'LL BE THERE FOR YOU" - FLOOR

9798497047042

NEVER BE ASHAMED OF YOURSELF (THAT'S YOUR PARENTS' JOB)

9798497735581

I'M 99% ANGEL, BUT DON'T ASK ME ABOUT THAT 1%

9798497047011

I NEVER ARGUE BUT I EXPLAIN WHY I AM ALWAYS RIGHT

9798497052176

MY CRAZY IDEAS & HORRIBLE DRAWINGS

9798497057188

PEOPLE I WISH I COULD PUNCH IN THE FACE

9798497057041

BORN TIRED

9798497771053

BIRTHDAY GIFT

HAPPY BIRTHDAY
JUST LET ME KNOW HOW OLD WE WILL TELL PEOPLE YOU ARE NOW
9798757794709

ANOTHER YEAR OLDER
9798757794655

I HOPE YOUR BIRTHDAY IS AS FANTASTIC AS I AM
9798757794594

YOU OLD FOSSIL
9798757639673

GIFT FOR FRIENDS

LIFE IS BETTER WITH **FRIENDS**
9798757576312

YOU ARE MY FAVORITE *Bitch* TO BITCH ABOUT BITCHES WITH
9798757576350

THANKS FOR ALWAYS PULLING MY FINGER
9798757576459

WE WILL REMAIN BEST FRIENDS FOREVER, BECAUSE WE'RE TOO LAZY TO MAKE NEW **FRIENDS**
9798757576404

APPROPRIATE TO GIFT ON DIFFERENT OCCASIONS

HAPPY ANNIVERSARY
9798758202500

ANOTHER SUCCESSFUL YEAR OF NOT MURDERING EACH OTHER
9798758202494

YOU = AWESOME
9798758419724

I DON'T CARE THANKS
9798758397220

GET WELL SOON AT LEAST YOU DIDN'T DIE
9798758290248

life IS TOUGH BUT SO ARE YOU
9798758290309

THANK YOU
9798758389874

I'M LOOKING FORWARD TO ANNOYING YOU FOR THE REST OF OUR LIVES
9798758243039

FOR WORKPLACE, BOSS, COWORKERS

THINGS I WISH I COULD SAY AT WORK BUT CAN'T

9798757110158

NOTES FROM ANOTHER UNNECESSARY MEETING THAT COULD HAVE BEEN AN EMAIL

9781706341345

TEAM AWESOME

9798757019086

ANOTHER DAY AT WORK OF OUTWARD SMILES & INWARD SCREAMS

9798757101286

Best BOSS Ever

9798757127644

BOSS Lady

9798757127835

BOSS LADY

9798757127972

BIG THANKS FROM THE TEAM

9798757127729

GO AHEAD FIND SOME BETTER COWORKERS THAN US!

P.S. WE WILL MISS YOU !

9798756868296

I STARTED THINKING OF YOU AS FRIENDS FOREVER BUT YOU ARE LEAVING ME TO DIE IN THIS Shithole THANK YOU, Bitch

9798756868302

SOMEONE ONCE SAID "I AM OUTTA HERE " AND THEN LIVED A HAPPY LIFE EVER AFTER

9798756868326

GOOD LUCK FINDING BETTER COWORKERS THAN US!

P.S WE WILL MISS YOU A LOT!
P.P.S WE TRULY MEAN IT!

9798756873764

DON'T LEAVE ME ALONE WITH THESE ANNOYING PEOPLE

9798756984941

GOOD LUCK IN YOUR NEW JOB YOU TRAITOR

9798756984989

MORE THAN A TEAM WE ARE FAMILY

9798757021102

WHO SAYS I AM BOSSY? I JUST MAKE SUGGESTIONS WITHOUT OPINIONS

9798757101491

COLLEGE RULED & WIDE RULED COMPOSITION NOTEBOOKS

Notebook · 9798479673535

Notebook · 9798479673559

Notebook · 9798479673573

 9798478330040

 9798478102210

 9798478301088

 9798479471452

 9798478355883

 9798479501692

 9798479507205

 9798480084504

 9798480825671

A PERSONAL MESSAGE FROM THE PUBLISHER

First of all, thank you for your purchase. I know there were good number of choices for you, but you picked this one and for that I am extremely grateful and I really mean it.

I am a father of a kid and run a very small publishing business. You know, publishing has become very expensive these days but believe me, I tried hard to keep the price affordable, without compromising on quality.

IF YOU HAVE BOUGHT THIS BOOK FROM AMAZON AND THEN ENJOYED AND FOUND SOME BENEFITS IN USING THIS, THEN PLEASE POST A REVIEW ON AMAZON. (IF POSSIBLE WITH PICTURE/VIDEO).

Your feedback, opinions and advice will immensely help this small publisher to create better products. You can find some of my other publications like How to Guides, Journal, Planner, Guestbook, Children's Book, Coloring Book, Logbook, Tracker etc. under 2 author names at amazon. They are:

1. Creative Catalog
2. Smiley Kiddies

As you have seen in the previous page, please search both author names/brands in that way to get all our exciting books. EVEN, IF YOU HAVE ANY PERSONAL REQUEST THEN EMAIL ME at **creativecatalogpress@gmail.com**

I will try to produce your desire book for you. Wishing you all the best in your future success!

R.R.

Made in the USA
Monee, IL
16 December 2021

85585144R00063